ACHIEVER OF GOALS

OVERCOME A DEFICIENCY OF WILLPOWER AND MOTIVATION

By Daniel C. Thompson

If you have a dream, don't just sit there.
Gather courage to believe that you can
succeed and leave no stone unturned to
make it a reality.

Never give in, never give in, never, never,
never, never-in nothing, great or small, large
or petty – never give in except to convictions
of honour and good sense. Never yield to
force; never yield to the apparently
overwhelming might of the enemy.

Table of contents

Chapter 1

Self control

Self-control is a word we often hear mentioned in discussions of health and wellness. Often, we think about it when it comes to stopping a behavior we dislike, like eating junk food, or in the context of managing a feeling like anger. However, the true definition goes beyond these ideas. Here is the true meaning of the word self-control and how you can master it for yourself.

Self-Control Defined
he definition of self control is the ability to exercise restraint or control of one's emotions desires and impulses. In other words, we can prevent ourselves from doing something we don't want to do or from feeling something we don't want to feel, especially when we're tempted.

Additional words that may be used interchangeably for self-control include self-discipline, will-power, composuraint.

Possessing self-control is an incredibly helpful skill. It helps us to move from having the knowledge of what would be good for us and actually put it into practice. For example, when a doctor urges a patient to lose weight, self-control prevents them from eating too much junk food. More examples of displaying self-control include going to the gym instead of staying home to watch TV, or getting started on a project early instead of procrastinating.

Although we learn to self-soothe as babies (by, for example, sucking on a pacifier), we're not born with self-control. We develop this skill throughout our childhood and arguably our entire lives. This is why it's not unusual to see an upset toddler throw a toy across the room, but the same behavior would be bizarre in an adult.

Sometimes, however, individuals reach adulthood with too little or too much self-control. Neither situation is ideal. In addition to the physical and emotional challenges this might bring, too little or too much self-control can also have social and mental effects like isolation, depression, or anxiety. You might be wondering what a healthy amount of self-control looks like, but to best understand that, it's important to know what too much or too little looks like first. We'll start there.

Signs Of Too Much Self-Control

The ability to remain in control of one's emotions desires and actions is usually a quality that people admire. However, when someone possesses too much self-control, they can struggle. Sometimes, people suffering from excessive self-control come off as perfectionists or seem overbearing.

Experts call this behavior "overcontrol." Someone dealing with "overcontrol" might experience the following:

 with too much self-control don't stand out as much as those who lack self-control. Why? Because their behavior is often associated with positive words or characteristics, like hard-working, introverted, or highly sensible. With that in mind, how do we know if someone has too much self-control or is simply mature? Well, it depends on the individual.

If someone's behavior works for them and causes little to no distress, it's likely that everything is fine. However, if excessive self-control makes their physical, mental, emotional, or social life a challenge, they may benefit from seeing a licensed counselor.

How To Have Self-Control

Everyone has a different amount of self-control, and it can vary by situation, too, but most of us could use a boost to find a better balance between too little and too much. Here are a few tips to get you started.

Relax

It can be hard to have self-control when we trick ourselves into thinking something must be done urgently or stopped immediately. We also struggle with self-control when we're driven by our gut reactions. Imagine you're driving down the road at high speed, and a slow driver cuts you off. Your gut reaction is what makes you want to honk your horn and scream at them or worse.

To give yourself the best chance at a calmer response and a better day, learn to slow your thoughts, so you can postpone your gut impulses. Relaxation can help. Meditation, deep breathing, and mindfulness are all excellent ways to practice relaxation. The more you relax, the more likely you are to calmly approach stressful events and choose thoughtful responses instead of acting on impulse alone.

Learn To Plan

Self-control is hard to achieve without direction. For example, if you want to lose 10 pounds, and therefore need to skip your nightly dessert, it helps to plan ahead. Instead of hoping you'll be strong enough when the time comes, think of ways to curb your appetite in advance, so you're more likely to succeed.

To avoid relying on willpower, make a plan for what you will do the next time you're tested. Perhaps you can plan on doing 15 minutes of yoga or reading a good book when you have a craving for sugar. Using distractions like this can help you improve your self-control in the long run. You will eventually learn that you can manage unpleasant feelings and that you don't need to act on all of your desires.

Find Out What You Want

Sometimes we lack self-control because we're not clear on exactly what we want. For example, if it feels like you're going nowhere in your current job, make sure it's not because you don't know where you want to go next. When you have a clear goal, it's easier to exercise self-control because you can focus on making choices that point you in the right direction. A licensed therapist can help you figure out exactly what motivates you, and can be a powerful tool in helping you reach your goals using self-control.

That said, it's important to have goals that are meaningful to you. Do not set a goal just because someone or something else pushes you toward it. Look deep within yourself, and find out why your goal matters to you. If it doesn't mean anything to you, it will be very hard to dedicate yourself to it.

Role-Play

If practicing self-control is a challenge for you, role-play with a friend, a family member, or a therapist. This will help you confront your feelings in To start, think about a simple situation where you typically struggle with self-control. As your self-control improves, branch out to more difficult or challenging situations.
Importance Of Self-Control
Let's Look At An Example To Understand

The Importance Of Self-Control.

Say You Have A Project Deadline The Next
Morning. But Your Friends Invite You At
The Last Minute To Go Out For Dinner.

You're In A Dilemma. You Want To Go Out
And Have Some Fun With Friends. But, At
The Same Time, You Know You Should
Wrap Up Your Project So That You Don't
Have To Pull An All-Nighter.

What Do You Do?

You Exercise Self-Control. In Other Words,
You Don't Give In To The Temptation To Go
Out And Enjoy, And You Finish Your Project
Instead.

This Is How Understanding The Importance
Of Self-Control Plays A Vital Role In
Helping Us Succeed In Life.

There Will Always Be Things That Tempt And Distract Us From Our Goals And Commitments. It Is The Awareness About The Importance Of Self-Control That Drives Us Towards Making The Right Choices. Our Goals Require Our Unwavering Focus And Commitment, And Self-Control Is The Mechanism That Stops Us From Deviating From Our Path.

All Of Us Face Such Choices Daily. However, Many Of Us Can Exercise Self-Control And Ignore The Temptation To Break Our Resolutions. Self-Controlled Individuals Always Focus On Their Goals.

But Not Everybody Is Successful At Exercising Self-Control.

A Student Might Decide To Go Out For A Game Of Football And Skip His Homework. Or An Executive Might Use A Short-Cut To Save Time On A Project That Compromises

Its Quality Because She Finds The Work Tedious.

People Who Struggle With Self-Control Might Struggle To Meet Their Goals Sometimes. Self-Control Is The Magic Pill That May Taste Bitter But Delivers The Desired Results.

Benefits Of Self-Control

Self-Control Can Help You Hone Your Leadership Skills And Live A Happy And Fulfilled Life. Here Are Some Benefits Of Self-Control:

1. Decision-Making Ability
One Of The Benefits Of Self-Control Is That It Makes Decision-Making Easier. For Instance, A Person Might Love Chocolate But High Blood Sugar Levels Will Force Them To Exercise Self-Control And Stay Away From The Chocolate Bars, Cookies, And Desserts.

2. Greater Chances Of Success
A Person Who Has Self-Control Doesn't Get
Distracted Easily. This Enables Them To
Manage Their Time And Resources Better.
They Tend To Make Sustained And Focused
Efforts Toward Their Goals, Which Are
More Likely To Result In Success.

3. Self-Control Can Beat Temptations
Among The Benefits Of Having Self-Control
Is The Ability To Beat Temptation. Quite
Often, We Can Get Tempted To Do Things
That Divert Us From Our Goals And Affect
Our Quality Of Life.

For Instance, If We Don't Exercise
Regularly, We Will Not Only Face Problems
In Later Years Of Life But Also Regularly
Experience Aches, Fatigue, And Various
Other Health Problems.

4. Self-Control Can Make You Excel
Another Advantage Of Self-Control Is That
It Helps Students Perform Better In Exams
And Stay Mentally Sharp. They Are More
Focused On Achieving Their Goals Than
Their Peers.

Similarly, People With High Amounts Of
Self-Control Can Channel Their Time And
Energy Into Being Productive In The
Workplace, Which Leads To Success At
Work.

5. Better Personal Relationships
Self-Controlled People Are Not Only In
Charge Of Their Actions– They Can
Regulate Their Emotions As Well. They Can
Control Their Anger Or Harmful Emotions
Like Jealousy Or Hatred. This Helps Them
Handle Personal Relationships Better Than
Those Who Don't Have Much Self-Control.

Chapter 2

Control your emotional and Discipline your mind

Emotions are a natural and wonderful part of life. They color our world, help guide us through life, and give us insight into our inner thought processes.

But what happens when our emotions feel like they're controlling us instead of the other way around?

Overwhelming emotions can result in emotional blow-outs, damaged relationships, and poor life decisions. Although it takes some practice, anyone can learn to better control their emotions and use them in more productive ways.

mindset
Appearing in everything around us, there
are two parts: ourselves and the matter to be
dealt with. On the one hand, there is the
situation and our attitude towards the
problem. But on the other hand, our attitude
towards life will determine life's attitude
towards us.

We all want to grow. A growth mindset can
massively transform how we live our lives,
from how we think about ourselves to what
we want to accomplish. A growth mindset is
when you believe you can develop your
abilities, become your thoughts and
transform your life.

Have you accepted something in your life
that is not exactly what you wanted? Are you
attached to a past period in your life? Has

your imagination gone out the window? Many people in this world live their lives thinking that life is the way it is and accepting it. They have no idea how to change their life, get out of the rut or produce the results they are looking for.

How To Control Your Emotions And Discipline Your Mind

Have you ever lost your temper or peace of mind? Do you wish you could control your emotions and discipline your mind to work for you?

Well one of the best ways to boost mental energy is to recognize a fact that we are never taught: You have the power to choose how you feel.

Its so simple but the majority of people grow up being emotionally pushed and pulled around by whatever and whoever they come up against.

But by training your brain to think differently, you can choose how to feel and react to people and situations, and even improve mental and physical health for the better.

Build Mental Muscle
But it's not about just thinking positively. Or suppressing or ignoring emotions.

It's about learning how to think realistically.

Because our feelings are actually signposting what we need to focus on and we can even learn how to use their energy to work for us.

But one thing to remember is that because we all have different life experiences, we are all triggered by different things.

For some, the loss of a job is stressful or for others it might be the threat of war. Many of

us are triggered by conflicts with colleagues
or a spouse.

So any treatment or methods we use have to
be completely personal.

And emotional discipline is not a
one-size-fits-all process.

So it's important to develop coping methods
dependant to each person's needs, so that
they can deal with their unique challenges in
a healthier way.

Signs of emotional distress

If you're struggling with emotions, you
could be struggling any of these symptoms:

Feeling anxious, irritable, or depressed
Frequent conflicts at work or with family
Persistent unhappiness
Trouble sleeping
Unexplained health problems

1. Reframing
Reframing lets us view something in a new way, turning a negative into a positive.

And it helps us use whatever life hands us as opportunities to be taken advantage of, rather than problems to be avoided.

For instance, 1 person who is struggling to get a job after going for lots of interviews could take that really personally.

They can slip into long periods of depression and unemployment after going for a interviews and not getting a job.

But another person could reframe the same situation as a sign that the companies they interviewed with were obviously not a good fit for them and soon enough the right one will come along.

This way of looking at the issue, not only keeps emotions stable but the person who reframes this situation, would also walk into every interview feeling a lot more up beat and confident.

2. Improve Self Talk
The conversations you have with yourself have a direct impact on how you feel and how you behave.

And if your self-talk is filled with self-doubt, harsh criticism, and catastrophic predictions, you'll struggle to reach your goals.

But don't blame yourself for persistent negative self talk.

Because 95% of self talk has been shown to be subconscious.

And it's often the result of perceptions we have of ourselves from intense childhood or even adult experiences.

Do you call yourself names? For instance I had a client who used to call himself stupid idiot again and again.

Or do you talk yourself out of doing things where you might fail?

Well one way to reverse self criticism is to consciously develop positive personal mantras that you can use to talk back to the negative messages.

Repeating things like, 'I'm more than enough and always will be' or "I'm doing my best" tunes out the negativity.

And as the mind learns by repetition, over time, you'll grow to believe those statements more than the unhealthy things you've been telling yourself.

And this is one of the most powerful ways to control your emotions and discipline your mind.

3. Question The Belief
One of the rules of the mind it keeps you safe.

And to do that, your mind is hardwired to move you away from pain and towards pleasure.

So when it tells you that you can't possibly get a promotion or that you'll never be able to lose 10 pounds, it's because those things are hard.

But rather than listening to your mind, look at it as a challenge.

Get into the habit of doing the things you don't want to do.

Challenge yourself to keep applying for promotions despite your brain's insistence you won't land a new position.

But tell yourself that you love it, that you love looking for jobs. Because it means that you're progressing your life and progressing your career.

Or if you're running a marathon and you tell yourself 'Oh I hate this, it's so boring', you're not going to finish it.

You have to go, I love it, love it, I love it, even when it isn't true and that's how you collaborate with your mind.

So fool your mind into making the unfamiliar, familiar.

And each time you prove your negative predictions wrong, over time, you'll train and collaborate with your brain better and better. And believe in yourself and get what you want.

4. Use An Attack To Your Advantage

So if you know anything about Michael
Jordan and seen his interviews, he always
talks about what motivates him to perform.

And it's often an argument or what he's
perceived as an attack from an opponent.

Well this ties in with the method of using an
attack to your advantage.

Which means you don't fight the attacker
but you redirect their energy to accomplish
your goal.

So rather than resisting an emotional attack,
you use its energy toward a solution.

Because we're usually tempted to push back
or defend ourselves.

But instead you can use the force of a
conflict to serve your goals.

View the criticism as a potential solution, recast the attack as an attack on the problem rather than on you.

Use the energy as a motivator to move you forward and achieve your goals relentlessly.

5. The Art Of Detachment
Detachment simply means keeping yourself centered.

And it's really powerful because it keeps you strong in your sense of identity and wishes, regardless of other things and people.

It means you remain free from the influence of other people and events.

And focus your attention on what you want. So it's also a way of putting yourself first.

But it doesn't mean that you can't love or have empathy for others.

It just means that rather than being drawn in to drama or worrying about what other people are thinking,

Detachment gives you perspective, and keeps your thoughts under control.

You stay detached from a specific outcome, like getting a job or the pressures of finding a girlfriend or boyfriend.

And you don't get as swayed by the highs of the achievement, or the lows of the failures.

You remain level headed.

In fact, you don't even worry about what happens, and instead, you feel more content and enjoy what you're doing or whatever project you are working on.

Chapter 3

Adapt and overcoming challenge

Even though many of us hope for a carefree life, it just will not happen. Challenges will always be on our path. Sometimes, it may seem as if the walls ahead are simply too high to surmount. Yet, overcoming challenges is a part of how we learn and grow. Indeed, obstacles give us an opportunity to become the best versions of ourselves.

History is filled with examples of people who learned how to trounce impediments and develop psychologically from the process.

Take Demosthenes, for example. He is now recognised as the greatest of ancient Greek orators. Nonetheless, when he was young, he had a severe speech impediment. He overcame this barrier through a self-designed, disciplined practice.

Einstein is another famous example of how overcoming obstacles can result in greatness. Apart from not speaking until he was three, he constantly faced doubt and under-appreciation by adults throughout his childhood and youth. Still, he found a way to develop his talents and become one of the most recognised names in human history.

In this article I'll explain how you can perceive overcoming challenges as a means of psychological growth. I'll explain why we need to fight the obstacles we face — and why we need to do it adaptively. Finally, I'll give you eight science-based tips for overcoming obstacles in a way that helps you grow and become braver and more confident.

Why you need to overcome obstacles

The examples from the introduction illustrate something that is called overcompensation in psychology. When we have an actual or perceived deficit of a sort, we will usually try to offset it by developing it into a particular forte. This strong point will then serve as a counterweight to the shortfall.

Overcompensation means going above and beyond what is necessary. Demosthenes could have merely fixed the speech impediment and lived an average life. But no. He became the greatest orator.

Examples of overcompensation reveal how overcoming challenges opens the path to psychological growth in life. Albeit going that far is not necessary for every obstacle we face, we must say that avoidance is usually maladaptive (or unhealthy).

When we face hurdles, we are presented with a choice. We can either commit to overcoming challenges — or to failing or stagnating. Here's why.

When you avoid dealing with difficulties, you risk experiencing a range of adverse emotions. Some of the most common ones are anger (for your aspirations remaining unfulfilled), guilt (because you know that you did not try hard enough), or envy (when you witness others getting what they want).

You are also bound to become stressed because problems rarely just disappear. Avoidance of difficulties, research reveals, leads to a diminishing sense of control. In turn, your psychological well-being and mental health will decline. Ruminations are excessive, repetitive thoughts that make it impossible to think productively about anything else. Rumination is tied to avoiding dealing with different life issues.

Overcoming challenges: tips
How we respond to complications is highly individualised.
It could be affected by our past experiences, mental habits, as well as our personalities. Seeking and overcoming challenges seems embedded in some people's temperament and personality structure.

Nonetheless, whether we are naturally geared towards adventure or not, we will hit an impediment here and there.

 Overcoming obstacles will be easier if you incorporate some of the following tips on productive coping with challenges.

1. Analyse the problem well
It may seem obvious, but the first step to overcoming challenges without difficulty is understanding the problem ahead. Still, many of us fail to approach the issue analytically. You may be amazed by how

often we succumb to apprehension, avoidance — or daydreaming and unsubstantiated optimism, on the other hand — instead of scrutinising the problem critically.

Therefore, examine where the problem truly lies. Is it a real or perceived obstacle? Which aspect is the most important one? In what order do you need to tackle the elements of the difficulty? What is it that you can and cannot impact? What resources do you need — new knowledge and skills, others' help, time, or determination?

2. Consider it an opportunity, not a threat
A common obstacle to successfully overcoming challenges is our mindset. I will be the first to admit that I'm not the type of person who goes about looking for challenges and adventures. Even more concretely, I used to feel threatened by any new and tricky situation. Still, what I found very useful is changing my perspective.

What may not come naturally to you could be developed through practice.

"The first step to overcoming challenges without difficulty is understanding the problem ahead. Still, many of us fail to approach the issue analytically."

Those who enjoy challenges — and thrive facing hitches — see every obstacle as an opportunity to become greater, better, different. You, too, can train your mind to think of hindrances as a chance to learn something new and evolve rather than to suffer.

3. Examine and dismantle your self-doubts
Overcoming obstacles is often made more difficult by your own unhelpful thoughts, especially if you're used to avoiding facing challenges. When you look at your records and see but a few instances in which you fought a problem head-on, it's easy to succumb to self-doubt.

Doubting your abilities, or even loathing yourself for lack thereof, will get you nowhere. What you need to do is to examine and knock down your lack of faith in your skills. Where does it come from? What thought comes to your mind when you anticipate trouble? How does it make you feel? How realistic is such a belief? Could you think about the situation differently (hint — yes, you could)?

4. Keep a record of your past successes
One helpful way to deal with self-doubt more effectively is to document one's successes. Many people tend to overestimate their shortcomings. At the same time, they underestimate how well they can address problems. As a result, their self-perception gets distorted, making them blind to their abilities.

Make a CV of your past accomplishments. Do not hold back but praise yourself for everything you achieved. Remember the times when you overcame snags with triumph. What qualities did you need to mobilise to overcome challenges? Write them all down. And then, come to this "CV" whenever you feel a lack of confidence creeping on you.

5. Make a solid plan
Once you are clearer on where the problem lies, what unhelpful thoughts might be hindering your success, and which talents you can rally to help you in overcoming challenges, it's time to plan how to do it. In other words, you are highly unlikely to accomplish your goals if you do not combine a belief in yourself with a solid action plan.

Define the goal and communicate it to those who need to be involved. Make a step-by-step map of action that is clear and easy to follow. Make sure there are tangible steps and smaller objectives on the way to the final goal. Measure the results — and celebrate them, too.

6. Assemble a circle of support
Overcoming obstacles is much easier when you have someone to lean on. Social support has been confirmed to be one of the crucial factors in psychological well-being over and over again. Somehow, life problems tend to seem much bigger when you feel alone in dealing with them.

7. Meditate
Meditation is a technique that can help you integrate the tips we have spoken about above. Meditative practice teaches you to calm your mind and free it from ruminative apprehensions and adverse emotions. It gives you the mental flexibility and physical tranquillity you need for overcoming obstacles with success. Finally, after meditation, you will notice greater clarity in understanding the problem ahead and how you can tackle it.

8. Pledge to self-care
Let me be straight — overcoming challenges can be hard work. It's easy to disregard healthy habits when you are entangled with problems. This is why you should commit to a self-care practice and ensure you are well cared for.

Ways to Overcome Challenges in Life
1. Make A Plan
While you don't know what is going to happen in the future, you can always plan ahead. Look at the patterns in your life and see what challenges you've struggled with. Assess the optimal outcomes and make a plan for how you can achieve them.

If you work somewhere and can anticipate the types of challenges you may face, then you can plan ahead. This is the same for students in school. If a challenge is time management, then you can learn and plan for calendar management, for example.

2. Know You're Not Alone
Every person in this world has their low points. Some may handle or even hide it better than others. But the truth is, whatever you are going through, there are others who have been through it too. You're not alone. Try to reach out to your community and network. Speak your feelings and express your concerns in all settings of your life.

3. Ask For Help
You're not alone, so you can find help. There's no need to feel ashamed for asking for help. Whether you choose to rely on a loved one, a stranger, a mentor, or a friend, there are people who want to help you succeed.

4. Feel Your Feelings
By masking your feelings, they are not going to go away. Rather, feelings become trapped energy and can even have negative health consequences when they are

ignored. Take some time to feel what you feel. This could come in the form of meditation. Or, if you'd rather write down what you feel, writing can be a therapeutic and cathartic experience.

When you feel and share your feelings, you may also be able to see your situation in a new light. This exercise could lead you to come up with novel solutions and overcome any challenge at hand.

5. Accept Support
Asking for help is only one side of the coin. On the other side of the coin, you have to be open and willing to accept support. People who come to your aid truly do care about you. Be open to receiving help when you need it.

6. Help Others
The old adage goes, "What you give is what you get." If you've been through a situation or have advice for someone you know who

is going through a tough time, be sure to help out! Helping others not only benefits them, but it can also help you feel happier yourself.

7. Think Big

It can be easy to let yourself think small because of the fear of failure, or even the fear of making a decision. But, to accomplish great things in life, you have to be open to taking risks. With whatever challenges may arise, always think and dream big. That way, you will achieve more than you could have ever imagined. Try not to let your thoughts get in your own way.

8. Positive Mindset

What you think becomes your reality. Train your mind to think positively. This will take both time and practice. It begins with mental awareness. You can practice awareness through mindfulness techniques and meditation. When you get good at acknowledging your thoughts and letting them pass, you can stop negative thoughts in their tracks.

9. Don't Give Up

When a challenge arises, be it a big test in school or an upcoming running race, don't give up! Persistence is a huge key to overcoming challenges. Giving up means that you will neither overcome the challenge nor learn from it. Power through challenges by asking for support, feeling your feelings, and making a plan to work through it.

10. Work Smart, Not Hard

Generally, there is more than one way to get something done. However, there's always just one optimal way or best way of doing it. To work smarter rather than harder, start by working backward. Outline and define your goal. Then, plan the process for how to get there.

Chapter 4

Overcoming the lack of willpower and motivation

While many people hold tightly on to responsibility of their deficient willpower and for their not good enough preferences, it's quite obvious that they still haven't given up optimism or positive affirmation. Predominance still exists and that, willpower is something that could be well-read and can be modified.

Lack of willpower doesn't means that you are lacking in other aspects for getting a desired job and not just the cause which you might fall short to achieve your aims. The only thing is that you need to set up your inspiration for makeover and set a clear aim.

Second, you need to supervise your aims towards the desired job role. The third module is ofcourse determination to achieve them.

 At its fundamental nature, willpower is the skill to defend against short- term point of view with the purpose of come together with long term aims. And there are several good rationales to do so.

overcome lack of willpowerPut off convincing yourself that you can't do anything to achieve your job role before trying; but you never know how things will turn out when it does happen, you just need to go through a better sense that you were right to overcome from lack of willpower. It may resound dim, but it's extremely helpful in looking forward to.

Overcoming Lack of Willpower:

The following mentioned are few tips on how to increase willpower and determination and also self development techniques that help you improve willpower.

1. Don't keep yourself in a steady position when willpower collapses:

Sometimes candidates fail to attain this at the very first moment, it usually happens to the entry- level candidates since they are all the way new to the interview levels and facing the interviewer for the first time.

So it's quite imperative for them to stop themselves from exhausting from low self- determination power.

2. Employ your thoughts with mind's judgment:

A mind is an authoritative method for humanizing for a stable willpower while looking for dream job role. You need to focus more on the strongest points you have in your kitty while applying for a job. Capture best use of your mind, especially your inner thoughts. It could be really helpful for you to take a wise decision for your career in future. Opening of this wistful eye is somewhat very necessary for the self- improvement in career and better prospects in the employment sector.

3. Think about some superior plan:

First, prepare a superior plan to come out for improving lack of willpower. Without fail when you try to come over and hang around your real realization, think about the negative as well as positive strategy as an alternative. Here you can achieve the set goals and which you wish to have for your real job role. Whenever there is a need for a simple thought to frighten influence on your awareness, and then you surely consider about great satisfying plan.

4. Make good level of stress buster:

Habitually, this is not a mindful
alternative. To a certain extent,
candidates dig a way out from such old
practices limited to accept understanding
for the reason that they are in a harassed
situation. Candidates awfully looking for
job need to make their own way to drain
out all the stress level in order for
building willpower.

5. Take one footstep at a time:

Often, candidates give up on their career or dream job not because they lack in determination, but because they feel weighed down by the hugeness of the aim that they have to achieve. Let a good quality method to be compressed with this feeling of overcoming and crush those things down obsessed by various negative feelings and schedule the series of overcoming which assure you victory. You need to take a step forward in order to overcome from lack of willpower so that you can progress well in your future.

6. Planning of strategy to overcome from willpower lacking:

The magnificence of this stratagem doesn't only promise accomplishment; but it also assures that you will overcome from willpower lacking. Not at all, place yourself in a situation of determination weakening. As soon as you reach to your each aim for achieving your desired job role and work towards it, you will get a huge wisdom of happiness and satisfaction in yourself by making it much easy for you to deal with the subsequent one. When you arrive at the finishing target, you are further lying on your front to feel a good judgment of abundance and influence, moderately than the other insignificant distinctive reactions.

7. Be at your inner self:

It takes a huge quantity of attempts to hold back your typical individuality, preference, and actions. But when you set your mindset to achieve the particular job for your better career, doesn't matter how tough the path is. Not astonishingly, doing so will surely reduce lack of willpower. Candidates who apply this type of strength of willpower in order to delight others were more categorically exhausted than candidates who truly held to their own inner aims and needs. When it comes to determination level, some applicants find themselves low, compared to those candidates who feel sheltered and contented.

8. Never put down optimism:

If you ever assume that it doesn't work; or perhaps it won't work now, than you are not only lacking in willpower but you lack hope as well. You believe that it just since you have not done something like this in the past, so you can't even do it now in the present also. But publicize your mind's eye through which you have collected more knowledge by now and you can't predict whether something will work or doesn't works for you. But you must be the one who should not lose hope and willpower with the purpose of achieving your targeted job and remember, this is you who can only make it happen.

9. Initiate short- term ambitions:

Since when you will be capable to achieve little or can say short- term goals, you can rather move on to some superior and bigger achievable life goals, like applying for the type of industry or role you have always dreamt to work for, or following to the posts of that company's HR manager so that whenever there is a vacancy for the role you desire for, you can get notifications and apply immediately there. This is how you can start initiating the process of achieving by short term aims and jumps to achieve long- term goals.

10. Conversation is a good remedy:

When you need to overcome from lack of willpower and effectiveness, then there must be a discussion looking forth ahead to you. You can try discussing your problems or hitches which hold you back from the fear of giving interviews and/ or for applying. There must be somebody that could be very close to you and on whom you can really rely; talk to them in relation to your hopes and prospects and explain them with what you want and how you should move forward to achieve your goals of career so that they can guide you to overcome from willpower lacking.

11. Find out the affirmative side of change:

Changes eventually makes lives less tedious, permits us to know-how innovative things, makes us realize dissimilar standard of living and diverse points of view, gets us out of dilemma and refresh our minds, makes us more energetic and vigorous. Hence, you need to make a change and transform the plan to achieve your desired job role. Once you get to have the benefit of one main change in your life, you will be influenced to create other changes in your career. Change in plan will certainly brings a definite transform in your career and future as well.

12. Be more optimistic and stay encouraging:

First of all, you need to stop distressing that much about the whole lot of drained career due to lack of willpower and ideas that things won't wind up pretty well. Except this is only you can stay unbeaten, positive and act like the game has just begun to achieve the position you have desired for in the corporate world. Your actions will more habitually need to be stay tuned that could bring constructive results for you. You may not be the luckiest candidate around in the crowd of hundred applicants, but there are many ways to develop your strong willpower.

Self-determination is that capability to organize your opinions and actions with the aim of achieving several goals for your future and especially what efforts you are making to bring a change in your career. In other words, self improvement or the ability to go after your imaginings and do what you actually need desperately to achieve in your career. Try to gain willpower following your inclination and stay planned. Determination is a talent which you can increase only by getting yourself involved fully into it. The more you will be determined to achieve your desired place of job, the more you will have the benefit of it and find causes to put into practice it further. Don't give up your entire life and hand over it onto destiny; become conscious that all the renowned people in the corporate industry actually did something to become famous and tried hard to reach to the place where they are today. Make your mindset fully strong and enhance your willpower to achieve something in life.